Contents

Being a Referee

Andy Croft

Published in association with The Basic Skills Agency

Hodder & Stoughton

A MEMBER OF THE HODDER HEADLINE GROUP

Acknowledgements
Cover: Matthew Ashton/Empics

Photos: p2 Steve Bruce/Allsport; pp5, 8, Empics; p12 Gary M Prior/Allsport; p14 Hulton Getty; p21 The Observer/Hulton Getty; p25 Ross Kinaird/Allsport

Every effort has been made to trace copyright holders of material reproduced in this book. Any rights not acknowledged will be acknowledged in subsequent printings if notice is given to the publisher.

Orders; please contact Bookpoint Ltd, 39 Milton Park, Abingdon, Oxon OX14 4TD. Telephone (44) 01235 400414, Fax: (44) 01235 400454. Lines are open from 9.00–6.00, Monday to Saturday, with a 24 hour message answering service. Emails address: orders@bookpoint.co.uk

British Library Cataloguing in Publication Data
A catalogue record for this title is available from the British Library

ISBN 0 340 80071 2

First published 2001
Impression number   10 9 8 7 6 5 4 3 2 1
Year   2007 2006 2005 2004 2003 2002 2001

Typeset by SX Composing DTP, Rayleigh, Essex.
Printed in Great Britain for Hodder & Stoughton Educational, a division of Hodder Headline Plc, 338 Euston Road, London NW1 3BH by Redwood Books Ltd, Trowbridge, Wilts.

1 Why Be a Ref?

Everybody hates Referees.

Fans shout at them.
Players shout at them.
Managers shout at them.

Everyone blames the Ref
when their team plays badly.

Fans criticise them.
Players criticise them.
Managers criticise them.

People call Refs all kinds of names.

Sometimes people spit at and threaten the Ref.
Refs are sometimes pushed and punched.
Refs have even been murdered!

Nobody likes the Referee!

No-one remembers
when the Ref has a good game.
But everybody remembers
when the Ref has a bad game.

It's not always much fun being a Ref.
But every week 2 million people
play football in Britain.
That's a lot of games.

Every game must be fair.
Every game must be safe.
That's why every game
needs a good Ref.

2 Did You Know?

Here are some things that
you probably didn't know about Referees.

West Ham's Trevor Brooking
once bumped into the Ref.
It was an accident.
He knocked the Ref out.
No-one knew what to do.
So Bobby Moore blew the Ref's whistle.
The game stopped
and the Ref was carried off!

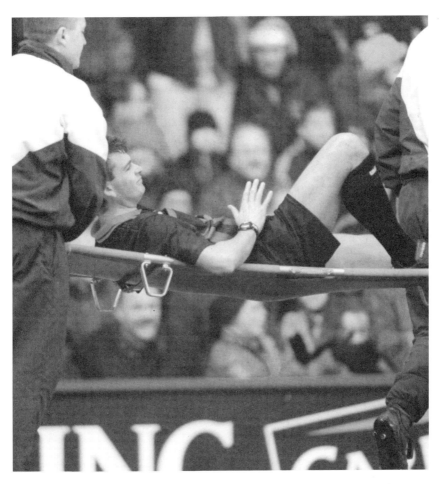

Even referees don't escape injury during football matches.

A Ref once scored the only goal
in a game between Plymouth and Barrow.
The ball bounced off his foot
and into the Plymouth goal!
He was very upset.
He gave the goal to Barrow!

In 1969 a Ref booked all the players on the pitch.
He even booked one of the linesmen!

In 1975 a Ref was getting ready for a game.
He heard one of the teams
singing in the changing room.
They were singing rude songs about him.
He marched into the changing room
and booked everyone,
including the subs.
The game hadn't even started!

A Ref once dropped his cards during a game.
Paul Gascoigne picked them up
and showed the Ref the yellow card,
just for a joke.
The Ref didn't think it was funny.
He booked Paul Gascoigne!

These days Refs have their own magazine.
They call it a Refzine (instead of a fanzine).

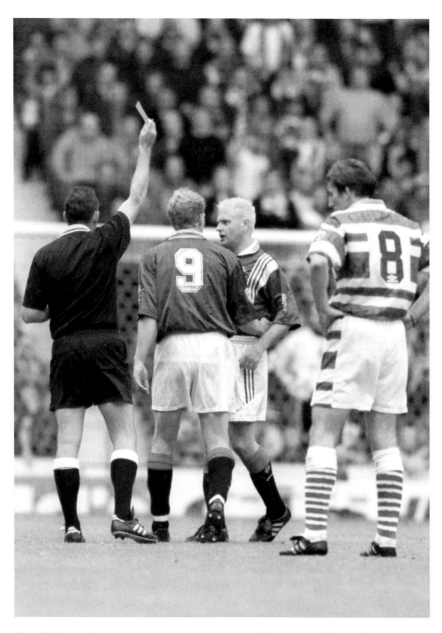

Paul Gascoigne was once given a yellow card just for making a joke!

3   Men in Black

There are lots of famous players.
There are lots of famous managers.
There are even famous fans.
But how many famous Refs do you know?

H.S. Barnlett is still the youngest ever
FA Cup Final Ref.
When he refereed the Final in 1914
he was only 32.

Major Francis Marindin
was the Ref in nine FA Cup Finals.
He was later President of the FA.

Stanley Rous invented a way to help referees.
It is called the diagonal system.
This helps the Ref to cover the game.
Instead of chasing the play,
the Ref runs up and down the pitch
from one corner to another.
Refs still use this system today.

Three English Refs have appeared
in the World Cup Final:
George Reader in 1950,
Bill Ling in 1954 and
Jack Taylor in 1974.

Many people think Pierluigi Collina
is the best Ref in the world today.

Some of the best British Refs today are
Mike Reed, Jeff Winter,
Graham Poll, David Elleray,
Uriah Rennie and Andy D'Urso.
Andy D'Urso once used nine yellow cards
and three red cards
in one match.
It's still the Premiership record.

Pierluigi Collina is one of the best Refs in the world.

4   History

The first Ref was used in 1867
in a game at Cheltenham College.
He was called the Umpire,
just like in cricket.

By the 1870s there were two Umpires at every game.
Each team brought their own Umpire!
They often disagreed.
Soon there was a third Umpire.
He was called the Referee.
His job was to sort out arguments
between the Umpires.

The Referee looks on as the captains of England and
Belgium shake hands before a match in 1924.

In 1891 the Referee was put in charge of the game.
The Umpires were called Linesmen.

In the 1930s the FA tried playing two Refs,
one in each half.
But there wasn't enough for them both to do.

These days there is too much for the Ref to do!
The Linesmen are now called Assistant Referees.
There is also a Fourth Official at professional games.
The Fourth Official has to
check the subs,
show how much injury time is left and
have spare balls ready.

In 1878 Refs started using whistles.
In 1976 they started using yellow and red cards.
Yellow is for a booking.
Red is for a sending-off.
This is so fans and other players
know what is happening.

In 1992 Premier League Refs
stopped wearing black shirts.

5   The Future

The Ref's job is hard.
It gets harder all the time.

Some people think
Refs should use video replays,
to check what has happened.

Some people think
there should be two Refs –
one in each half.

Some people think
Refs should be ex-players.

Some people think
Refs should be full-time.

Top Refs are now paid £900 a game.
If they referee well
they are paid a bonus.
But if they are not good enough
they are relegated
to the Nationwide League!

6   If You Were the Ref . . .

How well do you know the rules of football?
How good would you be as a referee?
Test yourself with these questions and answers.
Remember, the referee's decision is final.

Question:What do you do if the goal cross-bar
          breaks during a game?
Answer: Abandon the match.

Question:Can a defender step off the pitch
          to put the opposing forwards offside?
Answer: No, this is unsporting play.

Question:What do you do if a dog runs onto the
          pitch and stops the ball going in the net?
Answer: It's a drop-ball.

Question: Do you need flags on the half-way line?
Answer: No.

Question: What do you do if someone in the crowd
blows a whistle and a player picks the ball
up for a free-kick.
Answer: Award a direct free-kick for handball.

Question: If a penalty has to be re-taken
can another player take it?
Answer: Yes.

Question: What do you do if a player takes off a
shin-guard and hits the ball with it?
Answer: Award a direct free-kick for handball.

Gordon Banks goalkeeping skills came into action when there was a stray dog on the pitch.

Question: Can the goalkeeper take a throw-in?
Answer: Yes.

Question: What do you do if the ball is kicked into the goal from the kick-off?
Answer: Award a goal

Question: Can a player score an own-goal from an indirect free-kick?
Answer: No. You award the other team a corner.

Would you have been able
to make the right decisions?

7   Stuck in the Middle

It's easy being a Ref, isn't it?
Anyone could do it, couldn't they?

The Ref has to do the following things.

- Check that the corner-posts and flags are set up.
- Check the nets are secure.
- Make sure the ball is the right size and weight.
- Make sure there are spare balls.
- Toss a coin before the match
  to decide ends and which team starts.
- Keep the time.
- Add on time for injuries, subs and time-wasting.
- Enforce the Laws of the game.
- Start and stop the game.
- Make sure there are only 22 players on the pitch.
- Watch for the Linesmens' flags.
- Decide if a player is offside.
- Make sure defenders are 10 yards away
  when the ball is kicked.
- Award goals.
- Keep the score.
- Book players for misconduct or unsporting play.

- Send-off players for:
  violent conduct,
  serious foul play,
  foul or abusive language
  and repeated offending.

The Ref should give indirect free-kicks for the following actions.

- Kicking the ball out of the keeper's hands.
- Charging a player who does not have the ball.
- Charging the keeper.
- Coming back onto the pitch without permission.
- Arguing with the Ref.
- Unsporting play.
- Time-wasting.
- If the keeper picks up a back-pass.

The Ref should give direct free-kicks for the following actions.

- A handball or reckless tackle.
- Making contact with a player before the ball.
- Kicking, charging, hitting,
  pushing, spitting, holding,
  tripping up or jumping on another player.

Easy isn't it?

The Ref has to toss the coin at the start of the game.

8   Who Wants to Be a Referee?

There are 33,000 Refs in the UK.

Why do they do it?
Most Refs don't get paid.
They do it because they love football.
Because a good Ref
can help make a good game.

But it's hard being a Ref.

You need to be brave.
You need to be tough.
You need to be fair.

You need eyes in the back of your head.

You need to take hard decisions.
You need to ignore the crowd.
You need to stand up to players.

You need to be fit.

Players get a bit of a rest
every now and then.
But the Ref never stops running
for 90 minutes.
The Ref runs about 6 miles every game.

Every year thousands of people become Referees.
The FA run courses on being a Ref.
It isn't as easy as it looks.

You must be fit.
You must know the 17 Laws of Football.
You must pass an exam.
And you must have good eyesight!

You have to be aged 16–50 to be a Ref.
Or 14 and older if you want to referee Youth
Football.

Do you have what it takes to be a referee?

How to find out more

If you would like to know more
about becoming a Referee,
contact your local County FA.

The address and telephone number
will be in the phone book.

Or you can write to:
Referees' Department
The Football Association
16 Lancaster Gate
London
W2 3LW